Is Alcohol really the Problem?

Futurus Books

Is Alcohol really the Problem?

A COLLECTION OF OPINIONS TO
HELP UNDERSTAND AND WORK WITH
THE 12-STEP PROGRAMME

BY

CHRIS SHARPE

Dedication

To the many rooms of Alcoholics Anonymous throughout
the world and the thousands who occupy them, and
to those who give hope to the fear-filled newcomers who,
using their last ounce of courage, cross the threshold
looking for the promise of salvation.

First published in 2022 by Futurus Books
Copyright © Chris Sharpe 2022

ISBN 979-8-797-3-32480
Cover by Liz Bosley
Cover image by Polina Tankilevitch

Is Alcohol really the Problem?

A SELECTION OF OPINIONS TO
HELP UNDERSTAND AND WORK WITH
THE 12-STEP PROGRAMME

BY

CHRIS SHARPE

Why this book?

For me it all began years ago with a brief moment of enlightenment, a glimpse of sanity amidst the chaos of an otherwise insane day. I found myself blessed with a few seconds of rare clarity in which I could step outside of myself and contemplate the silence. I found a space where I could look inside and witness and consider the myriad thoughts which were racing through my mind. It took just those few precious seconds to realise that I was existing in a desperate alcohol-fuelled existence with absolutely no hope of a future, at least not without some dramatic change.

I can still recall the circumstances which surrounded those moments. They were desperate times when the choice could have gone either way, either suicide or a humble call for help. Fortunately I chose the latter and the following day found myself in a meeting of Alcoholics Anonymous. At the end of the meeting I was asked by a concerned member how I felt. I answered that I could now see the light at the end of the tunnel. I shall never forget the answer my concerned friend gave. He said, *'No, you can't see the light at the end of the tunnel but now you know where the tunnel is.'* This was an answer which filled me with uncertainty while at the same time gave me an endless supply of hope. Sometime later, with three or four years of sobriety, at a time when the 12-step programme was becoming part of my life, there came another one of those moments. This time I realised that I still had a brain only now it wasn't soaked in alcohol. My thoughts were clearer now, with hope foremost, choices more obvious and change unavoidable. It was then that I chose to go back to school as a mature student and then on to university. For once I was able to make choices that were calculable options and those choices laid the foundation for a new, bright and optimistic future. Alcoholics Anonymous and its programme had become a part of my life and although doubts and fears never left me, they were manageable now and much less of a burden.

So, for the last thirty years or so I have enjoyed the privilege of continuous high-quality sobriety. For the most part I have done my best to work with those who still suffer, through many happy years of being employed in residential treatment units, and later, continuing my work in private practice. Throughout my career I have kept notes, written worksheets, blogs and various assignments. I estimate that roughly 40% of the content of this writing comes from my studies, while the other 60% has been gathered from experience. It is those notes which make up the content of this book and it is my sincere hope that they will help others as they have helped me.

Chris Sharpe
Addiction Therapist
2022

You can either start at the beginning and read through to the end, or select a subject from the contents below, one which is of some personal interest or concern. The choice is yours.

Contents

The Despair of Addiction

A disheartened addict sat at the bottom of a pit, stranded in a pool of excrement, mostly of his own making. The pit was deep its walls sheer and unscalable. The excrement was cold, filthy and foul-smelling.

A man passing by heard the addict sobbing and peered down into the hole. *'I'll fetch you a ladder,'* he said, kindly.

'Wait,' the addict looked up at the man and asked, *'tell me first, what is it like up there?'*

'It's all right up here,' the man assured him. *'As far as I can see, everything is quiet and peaceful.'*

'Mmm,' the addict paused, doubting the unfamiliar. *'Thanks, but you can forget the ladder.'*

He shifted uncomfortably, looking down into the excrement which now came up to his waist. *'I'll stay here if you don't mind. The stink may be overwhelming and the atmosphere of this place unbearable, but at least it's mine. I know what it feels like and to be honest, I'm getting used to it now.'*

The passer-by scratched his head and went on his way.

The 12-step Programme of Alcoholics Anonymous

The 12-step programme of Alcoholics Anonymous is a treatment programme which, in the company of like-minded people, allows its members to achieve and maintain abstinence from alcohol. There are no dues or fees for AA membership; the organisation is self-supporting through peoples' own contributions.

1. We admitted we were powerless over alcohol – that our lives had become unmanageable.
2. Came to believe that a Power greater than ourselves could restore us to sanity.
3. Made a decision to turn our will and our lives over to the care of God as we understood Him.
4. Made a searching and fearless moral inventory of ourselves.
5. Admitted to God, to ourselves and to another human being the exact nature of our wrongs.
6. Were entirely ready to have God remove all these defects of character.
7. Humbly asked Him to remove our shortcomings.
8. Made a list of all persons we had harmed, and became willing to make amends to them all.

9. Made direct amends to such people wherever possible, except when to do so would injure them or others.
10. Continued to take personal inventory and when we were wrong promptly admitted it.
11. Sought through prayer and meditation to improve our conscious contact with God as we understood Him, praying only for knowledge of His will for us and the power to carry that out.
12. Having had a spiritual awakening as the result of these steps, tried to carry this message to alcoholics and to practise these principles in all our affairs.

The Serenity Prayer

The Serenity Prayer is the Alcoholics Anonymous prayer of choice, which is usually recited at the end of each AA meeting. The purpose of the prayer is to serve as a daily reflection on the association between inner peace and the blessed freedom from substance use.

Its origin is uncertain.

God grant me the serenity

To accept the things I cannot change.

Courage to change the things I can

and wisdom to know the difference.

Introduction

According to clinical studies, alcohol is considered to be the most harmful of drugs, due to its indirect effects, involving not only the user but also other people.

In modern times, the use of alcohol has become a way of life and as such has an ambiguous relationship with society. At its best alcohol can be a pleasurable, recreational distraction from the many cares and woes of modern life. At its worse, it is a much-maligned, misunderstood and costly social parasite, which has the extraordinary ability to destroy, not only the life of the user, but also those who care most for his or her wellbeing. Alcoholics Anonymous labels alcohol as *cunning, baffling and powerful,* meaning it can be the instrument of both pleasure and pain. Understanding its misuse, therefore, can, like the drug itself, often be a whirlpool of uncertainty and contradiction.

My own experience tells me that most practising alcoholics exist in a world of chaos and confusion. This could be mental, emotional and or physical confusion. In all probability there will also be chaos in relationships, family and social life, and even in the workplace. It follows, therefore, in my belief, that the suffering alcoholic must be offered sanctuary or some release from this chaos. They must be offered hope and refuge and a focus that becomes a point of hope.

Habitually it seems, and all too often to do with the emotion of relationships, we drink to excess to help forget about some other difficulty. This is more than likely learned behaviour and culturally what modern life encourages us to do. Sadly for some of us, this option all too often ends in failure. For example, while numbing painful emotions, excess alcohol in our system encourages neglected resentments to grow and fester. Furthermore the onset of inebriation causes the susceptible mind to be overcome by a host of hidden doubts and fears, as a consequence putting the drinker at great risk, and in danger of experiencing a further surge of those painful and dangerous emotions. As a result we begin to feel worse and illogically decide to drink more. Then, with the onset of intoxication, all rationality deserts us, we become impulsive, intolerant and unable to contain sane and rational reactions. If we are lucky we might end up being comatose, if not, we risk all hell breaking loose. Either way the consequences are usually chaotic, far outreaching the initial and soon forgotten impediment.

After the event, denial becomes the steadfast guardian of alcoholism. In the sober light of a new day it is easy to rationalise drinking by profusely apologising for the spate of unfortunate behaviour adding something like: *'I'm not really an alcoholic you know. Normally I can stop anytime I want to.'* With this unhelpful fabrication how can we honestly decide whether our drinking is truly out of hand or is, at best, running the risk of becoming a very serious problem? Most of us, as part of life's enthralling cycle, face countless stresses and strains which, if left untreated, go on to produce seemingly unmanageable mental and physical problems. Therefore it comes as no surprise that many of us see the ready availability of alcohol or drugs as a panacea or magic potion which, if we're lucky, results only in the shrouding of the initial problem or the suppression of uncomfortable or painful feelings for a limited amount of time. To the normal drinker, it quickly becomes obvious that excess use of alcohol creates its own uncomfortable and unmanageable problems, both inside and outside of relationships. Yet for the suffering alcoholic, the continuing use of alcohol becomes but another repeated and futile attempt to manage those painful and uncomfortable emotions, leaving the user with little to inspire or to help rise above the everyday problems of life. This poses the question: Is alcohol really the problem? Or is it merely a 'solution' to another mysteriously shrouded and long-buried issue? This is a question that I can't answer directly, but hopefully my experiences, as set down in the following pages, will go some way to explaining those deceptively insurmountable emotions in a way that can enable you to answer the question yourself.

Lostness

I remember asking a client new to recovery if she could describe in as few words as possible what she was feeling. After some careful consideration she explained that all she could feel was a sense of 'lostness'. I don't believe the word 'lostness' appears in the dictionary but it described so well what my client was feeling that I thought I would use it as part of the introduction to this book and add, in layman's terms, a short explanation.

Any chemicals which act on our brain and are 'mood altering' can become addictive and may lead to severe personality changes, resulting in what my client referred to as 'lostness'.

These potentially addictive drugs fall into two major groups: stimulants and depressives. Both groups serve to influence the chemistry of brain cells, so that changes in behaviour become apparent. These changes in brain chemistry go on to result in an abnormal disturbance of thinking as well as abnormal patterns of behaviour, and what we need to realise is that the we run the risk of the damage becoming permanent. So, allow me a moment to speculate!

If we accept that alcohol, drugs and/or any behavioural addiction can cause an extreme chemical reaction in the brain, and, if we then acknowledge that, through continued use, the enzymes which process these chemicals will most likely always remain abnormal, is it not then likely that we will always be susceptible (or addicted) to some sort of emotional high or low, if so, might I suggest that the feeling of 'lostness' is somewhere between complete chaotic drama and absolute hopelessness, leaving us abandoned without the comfort of any middle ground? If this is the case, what natural and healthy resources can we call on to combat this irrational feeling of 'lostness' and achieve an opposing state of emotional wellness?

There is counselling of course or therapy or a host of residential treatment centres both at home and abroad, all of which most require some financial outlay. Or we could consider joining support programmes such as Alcoholics Anonymous which has no dues or fees and which shows us how to achieve the reality of daily disciplines such as hope, gratitude and wellbeing. Or, we could return to the drama by taking another drink and completely numb our feelings for a short while.

The choice is always yours.

The Phenomenon of Craving

'It's the first drink that does the damage'

In simple terms there are two forms of craving: physical craving and mental obsession. Obsession is what happens before we pick up the first drink. Craving occurs after. Obsession is in our mind. Craving is in our body once we have chosen to act on the obsession.

The phenomenon of craving can be described as the reaction our physical bodies have to alcohol. For example, those who are addicted to alcohol find that when alcohol enters their bodies they experience an overwhelming compulsion to keep drinking.

With regard to the obsession, once we're established in the recovery process and there are no longer any addictive substances remaining in our bodies we can't experience physical craving, nevertheless, we may experience what is termed a mental obsession for drugs or alcohol. However these obsessions are not real. What we are experiencing is no more than a thought. So beware, because if we call it a craving then we might trick our mind into thinking we're doomed to fail once again. Instead, we need to call it a mental obsession, only then can we see it for what it really is. Remind yourself that if you do decide to drink or use, no matter how long you may have been free from the substance, once that substance is in your system, you will be right back where you left off.

To summarise, keep obsessive thinking in perspective and don't allow it to threaten you. While obsessive thoughts are most often negative and tend to be uncomfortable, remember that they are only thoughts and therefore projections, or false speculations. One final thing is to remind yourself that you are not alone. The Doctor's Opinion on page 30 of the Alcoholics Anonymous Big Book states:

'The idea that somehow, someday he will control and enjoy his drinking is the great obsession of every abnormal drinker. The persistence of this illusion is astonishing. Many pursue it into the gates of insanity or death.

We learned that we had to fully concede to our innermost selves that we were alcoholics. This is the first step in recovery. The delusion that we are like other people, or presently may be, has to be smashed.'

If you are unfortunate enough to experience a mental obsession, then I suggest that in the first instance you refer to the following:

- Stop and interrupt your train of thought
- Do something else or try to think of something else
- If the thoughts persist then see them for what they are and try to visualise them in a less threatening way
- It's always a good idea to communicate your thoughts to another understanding person
- If these thoughts persist, it may be advisable to, speak to a psychiatrist about anti-obsessive medications.

The Dilemma

**Only sobriety can alter the alcoholic's
insane reasoning process.**

A fundamental way to becoming part of the solution process is
first to be in possession of an awareness of the true problem. This
simple and obvious acknowledgement can change everything
and bring about the possibility of a reviving hope. However,
such an honest realisation can be difficult to grasp and may
need guidance from someone already involved in the process. A
casual observer might think that asking for help is easy enough.
Yet finding the willingness to reach out and do what someone
else asks us to do can at best appear challenging to some of us,
if not impossible. Why? Because the active alcoholic has so far
survived on a feeling of omnipotence, meaning they have become
masters of their own nonsensical universe to the point where
no one can tell them what to do. If a problem drinker shows a
modicum of willingness, tenacious addiction treatment centres
and persevering therapists will eventually demolish this myth,
mystically transforming their client into something completely
opposite. For once he does as he's told, he stays sober, goes to
several fellowship meetings a week, preaches the programme at
every opportunity, so much so, that over time his willingness
develops into something almost saintly. Then the need to be

analytical rears its head and it becomes time for the now ex-drinker to begin taking a long, hard look at himself and his past behaviour. This is the point where willingness takes a dive!

Try if you will, to imagine that initially the alcoholic brings with him into treatment, three pots or bags or maybe even shedloads of what the 12-step programme of Alcoholics Anonymous some-times confusingly terms as '*defects of character*'. For the sake of simplicity we'll call the first pot Pre-existing Problems. They consist of primary conditions such as trauma, abandonment, abuse, anxiety, low self-worth, emotional-deprivation and suchlike. The second pot contains the Addictive Substance, be it alcohol, drugs or maybe a behavioural addiction, any of which have been employed by the user to numb the Pre-existing Problems. The third pot is made up of the Direct Consequences of the addiction: problems with debt, work, health, relationships, self-loathing, past wrong doings and antisocial behaviour. Now, imagine that we take away the Addictive Substance in the second pot, through detox or even by going cold turkey, the contents of the third pot, because they are a direct consequence, will gradually fade away. All that remains are the contents of the first pot, trauma and anxiety etc which, with nothing left to numb them, are sure to come to the fore. This leaves the alcoholic with some good news and some bad news: '*The good news is they get their feelings back; the bad news is they get their feelings back.*' So goes a saying often heard in the meeting rooms of Alcoholics Anonymous. However it's a saying that's not quite as straightforward as it initially sounds

Vulnerability

'Hiding your real self from others'

For reasons which I don't fully understand, we live in a society where vulnerability can mean the same as being weak or susceptible to injury, and this is not quite correct. As a culture, we tend to believe that appearing emotional is a sign of weakness. For instance, we're taught at a young age to withhold our feelings in order to avoid painful experiences of shame. However, for the recovering addict, managing vulnerability requires being open, both emotionally and intellectually. Showing your vulnerability means you no longer have to suffer in silence, which in itself requires a certain amount of courage. It also means that you're acknowledging your own long-hidden weaknesses, allowing yourself to move forward. Only by allowing yourself to be vulnerable will you overcome your powerful ego and find the strength to follow a spiritual path.

Throughout our active addiction we tend to lock away our true selves and may be dishonest with people, especially those who love us most. In recovery, we are encouraged to surround ourselves with a fellowship of people who offer care and support. If we do this we will never be judged, either for showing our emotions or for crying when we need to cry. It's comforting to know that despite what the media tell us, there is much good in the world and people are often more compassionate than we might believe. Quality recovery offers the opportunity to form close bonds with those who will accompany us on our 12-step journey because quality recovery can't be achieved without you being open with regard to your vulnerability.

As the Serenity prayer states: *'The courage to change...'* is an essential aspect of the recovery process. Having the courage to be vulnerable in our relationships with others offers in return new solutions, a boost in confidence, and means we no longer have to fight our battles alone. The best part about sharing our vulnerability with others is the realisation that we are not the first person to do so. The process of sharing means we become connected with those who have gone before. Research professor, Brené Brown says: *'We can measure how brave you are by how vulnerable you're willing to be.'* She adds that she starts every day by putting her feet on the floor and saying, *'Today I will choose courage over comfort. I can't make any promises for tomorrow, but today I will choose to be brave.'*

Check out **Brené Brown's TED talk: The power of vulnerability** on YouTube.

Surrender

If addiction brings you to your knees, why not think about giving up while you're down there?

If like so many others you have suffered the ravaging consequences of untreated alcohol addiction, surrender can be the first step towards a new and worthwhile way of life, and should therefore be regarded as the platform upon which further, positive, recovery can be built. It's generally in early recovery that the defeated alcoholic is informed of the daunting prospect that without surrender there is little or no possibility for him or her to construct a new and sober life. I doubt any alcoholic would truly welcome the thought of complete surrender, mainly because their natural defence is to resist or deny the process and suffer the pain of those Pre-existing Emotions, in case they should be seen by others as weak or even cowardly. It sometimes seems to me as though the alcoholic is programmed in infancy to endure the fight even if they're convinced the fight is unwinnable. Therefore, under this dubious premise, they manage to survive for years believing the insane delusion that their addiction is not nearly as bad as the other person's. For this reason alone, I would suggest that to continue fighting is a nothing more than a desperate way of trying to hang on to an inflated ego while clinging to the erroneous perception of personal power over one's own life and the lives of others.

I hope by now that it's becoming clear that taking away the alcohol is relatively simple. The difficult part is learning how to manage those remaining emotional issues. However, the alcoholic should never, under any circumstances, accept or surrender to the physical disease of addiction alone. Such ready acceptance relates more to not trying, therefore leaving the addict resigned to certain failure. The still practising alcoholic will have no idea how powerful their disease can be until the desire for sobriety leads them to a place where they come to recognise their own powerlessness. I see surrender as being more of a state of mind where one waits impatiently for appropriate guidance. Delay in surrendering, if it occurs, is because, prior to recovery, problem drinkers are so used to trying to fix things themselves. They fall short because they are unable to recognise their emotional shortcomings and vulnerabilities.

On the positive side it's also worth noting that complete surrender can bring with it an intense feeling of relief. After an age of constantly struggling to maintain some semblance of sanity, plus the never-ending endurance of intense physical and emotional discomfort, it is hard to imagine the feeling of at last being able to let go and place the problem in someone else's hands, because if we are to succeed, that is what we need to do.

The Disease Concept of Addiction

The American Medical Association recognised alcoholism as an illness in 1956, based on the theory that excessive drinking and alcohol addiction is caused by a disease that affects the structure and function of the brain.

Let me try to explain what this means.

Treating substance abuse can be extremely complex and it's only right to question at the start what exactly we're dealing with. Is it a 'disease of the mind' or a 'family illness'? Is it what some call a state of 'dis-ease', or is it simply a straightforward, 'obsession or compulsion'? Or is calling it a disease just another way of being allowed to avoid the responsibility of doing something about it?

Whether an accurate description or not, initially the disease concept may not necessarily be a helpful way of defining your addiction, so let's consider for a moment that alcoholism can be caused by a combination of behavioural, emotional, environmental and biological factors, with a possible genetic risk factor thrown in for good measure. When we hear it said that alcoholism is a disease, we're not specifically talking about the behaviour of drinking or using. All the behaviour will do is identify the presence of an obviously painful, mood-altering disorder; because a disease is not something you do, it's something you have, meaning that technically the disease concept can be seen as little more than a theory of addiction. Similar to most illnesses, the signs and symptoms of alcoholism can vary considerably. So if a person's drinking is a sign of something that a person has, i.e. a disease, then we need to be clear about what that underlying something is. Therefore the first step must be abstinence or the complete removal of the masking substance or behaviour. Also important is the practice of communicating with other addicts so that we can identify with what is going on inside their heads in order to understand that what we have is not unique. So, the solution is relatively simple, try not to intellectualise your condition. Stay clean and sober, seek help, apply continuous action and effort and acknowledge the powerlessness of your addiction. That way you're at least in with a chance. Remember, it is not where we are now which is of the essence, rather it's where were going and what we intend to do about it.

The Recovery Process

A few words about Alcoholics Anonymous and its Big Book

Founded in the 1930s, Alcoholics Anonymous has become a primary support fellowship whose purpose is to carry its message to others. For this reason Alcoholics Anonymous provides a safe place for those who wish to discuss, or even debate their personal experiences with alcohol while having a genuine desire to overcome their alcoholism. Alcoholics Anonymous is a self-supporting organisation, it doesn't accept or seek financial support from outside sources and it strives to preserve personal anonymity at all levels.

Not knowing what is involved can be one of the biggest obstacles for a struggling alcoholic who is considering attending a meeting of Alcoholics Anonymous. Going to your first meeting can be challenging to say the least. If possible I'd suggest you phone the AA helpline first and ask an existing member if they can meet and greet you and guide you through your first AA experience. What is affectionately referred to as 'The Big Book' is the main text of Alcoholics Anonymous and lays out the 12-step recovery programme, as well as including the personal stories of those who have found recovery through embracing that programme.

Chris Sharpe

Despite growing knowledge and countless rehabs which also offer help and support, the success rate for the recovery of alcoholics remains disturbingly low, while relapse is high. It's my belief that denial (detailed later in this book), is one of the main reasons why it's so challenging to maintain quality recovery, and why it always has been and always will be. Nevertheless, the support system of AA has remained steadfast for more than 80 years, proving it to be a worthy advocate for those who have an earnest desire to be free of their problem. It might be worth you giving it a go!

If you take the time to read the first step of the Alcoholics Anonymous 12-step recovery programme you can't help but notice that it mentions the word, powerless. For me as an addiction therapist, this is a word which equates to a loss of, or lack of, self-control. The very nature of drugs and alcohol or indeed most behavioural addictions is that they supply the user with a source of instant gratification. This can be borne out by the late Carrie Fisher, who when discussing drug addiction in her confessional novel, *Postcards from the Edge*, wrote, *'The trouble with immediate gratification is that it's not quick enough.'*

At first sight the process of recovery can seem to be a long drawn-out procedure. Most treatment centres recommend at least 6 to 8 weeks of in-patient care, purely as a foundation, before recovery proper begins. In part this also helps to avoid the distressing prospect of early relapse. I'd also add that at times, insufficient self-control or the need for immediate gratification can be regarded as the root cause of relapse, but I suspect the problem is far more intricate than that. In my opinion, for behavioural or substance-abusing addicts new to recovery, relapse is better interpreted as a way of avoiding otherwise overwhelming emotional pain, but more about that later.

For anyone currently seeking help for their alcoholism, it's certainly worth bearing in mind that many professionals consider addiction to be an emotional illness: This being the case, a lack of self-control means not having the ability to appropriately restrain the painful emotions and impulses that create the need to drink. This complex loss of control can often be accompanied by, or blamed on, the inability to tolerate boredom long enough to concentrate on something positive, such as the recovery process. To complicate matters even further, consider that boredom merely means being left alone with your own feelings. Now there's a painful thought.

Regular counselling and/or regular fellowship meetings should therefore be considered as offering a valuable opportunity for the alcoholic to fully embrace the basics of the recovery process while at the same time minimising the risk of relapse. It must be reiterated here that confident and quality recovery most certainly takes time to achieve. It's also worth noting that the second step of the 12-step programme starts with the words *'Came to believe...'* This must mean encouraging the new fellowship member to 'enter the process'. If this is the case, then the word *process* might translate as a method of allowing the addict time to change and thus positively influence their future. Alcoholics Anonymous even goes as far as promising that the process happens, but augments this with a few words of caution: *'sometimes quickly, sometimes slowly...'* then adding, *'they [The Promises] will always materialize if we work for them.'*

As with any process, there are stumbling blocks, however. When considering engaging in addiction therapy it's worth noting that the process of change needs to be without the dubious indulgence of egotism or arrogance. If anything, the process of change needs to be about action, open-mindedness and willingness. I can assure you, it's far more rewarding to be part of the process by applying the needed action, than to be a cardboard cut-out sitting on the edge because you're either afraid or possibly because you believe you know it all while waiting for, and wanting, people to applaud the few achievements you believe you may have made.

The Alcoholics Anonymous 12-step programme grew out of the actions and experiences of the original members of Alcoholics Anonymous. The suggested programme has been designed as a way to help new members overcome their addiction to alcohol. This programme has not changed since its conception in the mid-1930s. It is my passionate belief that there is no right or wrong way to practise the programme other than with honesty, an open mind and willingness. As stated previously, recovery is a process, it's also about change and emotional growth and the 12-step programme is primarily designed to assist that change and growth. For a successful outcome, it's suggested that it is practised on a daily basis.

The 12-step Programme's Six Main Objectives

The details set out below are merely objectives, some of which are dealt with in more detail in subsequent chapters.

1. **Cognitive objectives.** Understanding ways in which your thoughts have been affected by drinking.

   The eclectic process of recovery should bring with it many important phases including empathy and the development of trust. Practising the programme is also a way of supporting the development of goals and linking them to action, primarily by promoting self-awareness. In his list of Therapeutic Principles, Irvin Yallom stated that: '... *self-understanding refers to the achievement of greater levels of insight into the genesis of one's problems and the unconscious motivations that underlie that behaviour.*'

   During the early process of recovery from active alcohol addiction, self- understanding, self-assessment or realising the ability to become self-aware, can be a sure way to discover unconscious, positive change. The cathartic challenge of working the programme in a group environment will aid the process of promoting a newfound awareness in the recovering alcoholic, enabling them to take a good look at themselves and their life and to discover what's working for them and what isn't. To become involved in the cohesive process of group therapy and sharing with others who have a common goal promotes a healthy awareness of oneself, while aiding the discovery that like everyone else, alcoholics are fallible human beings who possess both strengths and weaknesses. If managed well, this major cornerstone of recovery will most likely be accompanied by the realisation that strengths and weaknesses can be built on or overcome, as the case may be. In short, the therapeutic process of sharing with other recovering alcoholics plants the seed of change in the individual's conscious mind and inspires the drive and motivation to do things differently.

At this stage, the role of the 12-step fellowship becomes crucial in implementing what Yallom calls the genesis, and it is just that. The creation of a new, exciting and challenging prospect of behavioural change occurs once he or she has begun to develop empathy and trust within the relationship. From this new and challenging way of doing things, realistic and achievable goals will emerge. Also, a secondary but equally important function also matures: linking the goals to action helps the alcoholic to begin to take positive control of their affairs, where once, loss of control was a primary obstruction to recovery.

2. **Emotional Objectives.** Understand how your anger, resentment, lack of self-worth and so on can trigger using. Consider how you can otherwise manage these emotions.

'To forgive someone else is to forgive myself'

On the face of it, the above statement might appear unfair
or, at its best, unclear. Yet when we choose to indulge a
naturally negative response to another person's negative
action or behaviour inside our head, it inevitably turns
to anger and as a consequence the anger becomes resentment: trapped, annoying, ongoing and painful. I'd ask,
therefore, that you consider for a moment the motivating
prospect that to forgive might be a way of releasing from
the mind that never-ending loop of hurt. Complex though
it may initially seem, the difficulty of this exercise is not so
much about forgiving the other person but, by the grace
of God, more simply a case of forgiving ourselves and thus
becoming free to move on.

In other words, you can suffer the pain or alternatively
attempt to find peace of mind through the process of
self-forgiveness. Coupled with resentment, forgiveness is
a constant process, which carries with it its own rewards.

It interests me that the 12-step programme doesn't directly
mention the word 'forgiveness'. I believe this is because
true forgiveness is difficult, complex and complicated.
With regard to resentment, we must first be clear that
forgiveness is not necessarily about righting a wrong but
more about continuously relieving the torturous pain we
carry in our minds. For this we need to let go of the egotistical idea that we are acting in a superior way by forgiving
others, or that forgiveness is about being good and scoring
points or solving the problem.

We never completely solve, or become free of our problems, but with the aid of the 12-step programme we can hopefully learn how to manage them in a more efficient manner, or at least perceive them in a different and less challenging light, which is probable why step 9 of the programme uses the term, 'direct amends', rather than forgiveness.

Making direct amends involves the more humble process of taking personal responsibility for our own past actions, specifically those which have the effect of making the present unmanageable. Therefore we need to acknowledge that saying sorry to others, although humbling in itself, does not automatically connect with the current pain or with that of the past. For this we need to own our resentment because when it is triggered the pain is undeniably our own.

I'm suggesting that much of dealing with resentment is about looking within. As active alcoholics burdened with a fickle and sensitive self-worth, one of the main problems we face is the loss of self, or even looking for it elsewhere. Being in active recovery means the only place we can discover the true self is to look within ourselves, and we need an honest programme to do just that

3. **Relationship Objectives.** Understand your relationship with alcohol, drugs or addictive behaviour. Consider how the significant others in your life were encouraged into enabling.

Someone once wrote that co-dependency could be termed as the dysfunction in adulthood that grows out of the emotional deprivation experienced in childhood, which in turn leads to unhealthy, uncontrollable relationship issues, such as addictive/compulsive behaviour and self-destructive, self-seeking acts of personal and family destruction. More often than not, unhealthy co-dependency turns into an ongoing and dramatic battle of egos where all those involved endlessly rotate between positions of persecutor, rescuer and victim.

Co-dependency and family dysfunction become a problem when the family members become involved in unhealthy relationships with the alcoholic. Where one relies on the other for meeting their emotional and self-esteem needs, for instance. A relationship that provides one or both parties with the means to maintain their irresponsible, addictive, or underachieving behaviour can also be described as problematic.

Furthermore, a dysfunctional family is one where the addict or significant others often live in a state of anger, pain and shame, or chronic mental and emotional fear, all of which may be ignored or denied by an ongoing culture of blame. The many underlying problems of co-dependency and dysfunction frequently include addiction issues, which in turn can involve the misuse of alcohol as well as other abusive addictions.

The traits of co-dependent people can include:

- An irrepressible desire for drama in their lives

- An exaggerated sense of responsibility for the actions of others
- An over-sensitive reaction when their efforts aren't recognised
- A fear of abandonment or being alone: the co-dependent will do anything to hold on to a relationship or avoid the pain of being abandoned
- An extreme need for approval and recognition
- A sense of guilt when asserting themselves
- A compelling need to control others
- Difficulty identifying feelings

Poor boundaries and problems with assertiveness are also symptoms of co-dependency. Boundaries apply not only to the self but also to money, belongings, feelings, thoughts and needs. Co-dependent families experience a detrimental responsibility for other members' feelings and problems, or tend to blame their own dysfunction on someone else. Alternatively, co-dependents may develop rigid boundaries, becoming private and withdrawn, or occasionally they waver between the two.

Being assertive is a learnt skill. Co-dependent family members lose the ability to listen and communicate effectively with other members. Therefore they need to learn how to communicate their needs in a concise, direct and emotionally open manner. They also need to be aware of others needs as well as their own. Being assertive is important in improving family relationships as well as our own self-esteem.

The ongoing treatment of co-dependency can be complex, and treatment includes education and individual and group therapy through which co-dependents rediscover themselves and identify self-defeating behaviour. Treatment focuses on helping clients to get in touch with feelings that were buried during childhood: The goal of treatment being about clients experiencing their full range of feelings again.

4. **Behavioural objectives.** Understanding how powerful our addiction has been, and how it has affected our behaviour. Beginning to identify and use the resources available, which will help us to change through becoming active in using them.

In active addiction one of the more extreme delusions from which we can suffer is the misbelief that we are nothing more than physical beings defined by idealism and thus disconnected from the love of God. Someone once described this misconception to me as being more simply defined by the three 'S's: sex, social status and security. In relation to sex, stereotypically, this means that some men may believe it's more desirable for them to be seen with a beautiful woman and likewise, women with a handsome man. Social status can be demonstrated, for example, by possessing the latest model of a smart phone, a highly polished four-by-four, or maybe an expensive new show home, while in truth being mortgaged to the hilt. Perceived security is presented by showing off a wallet full of twenty pound notes while the bank account is grossly overdrawn. For the addict, struggling with the conflict of an inflated ego and damaged self-worth, all three of these illusions define a fabricated materialism designed to mask an otherwise solitary existence.

Therefore, one of the more profound and long-term goals of recovery is to remove ourselves physically, emotionally and spiritually from existing in this ego-driven insanity where success, physical attraction, power and material possessions profess to be the core elements of life. The true objective of the programme is that, instead of looking outside ourselves for conviviality and companionship, it asks that we should attempt to be more humble and search inside to discover where true joy can be found. In simple terms, we're talking about moving from isolation to inclusion, a process which can at first appear to be an odd contradiction, yet the Big Book of Alcoholics Anonymous promises that if we search inside of ourselves then we will be, *'Rocketed into a fourth dimension of existence',* and I'm all for that!

In technical terms, what we're discussing here is the nature and designs of the True and False self. English paediatrician and psychoanalyst, Donald Winnicott, said that *'The false self is a defence, a kind of mask of behaviour that complies with others' expectations.'* In contradiction, he defined the true self as: *'A sense of being alive and real in one's mind and body.'* We commonly call the false self a mask, which can be described as a protective veil we wear, a defence against external influences, or that which is aptly defined in the dictionary as an object normally worn typically for protection or disguise. Most recovering addicts will come to recognise being behind the mask as a cruel misrepresentation, a lonely place where we go to hide in order to prove to others that we're something we're not. So, armed with this information, the question we need to ask ourselves now is, where and how do we find our true self? Instead of continually perpetrating the lie, how do we search instead for something hidden deep within ourselves and in so doing, create a new, real and honest identity that some recovering people choose to call the love of God?

Like the substances or behaviours we once depended on, emotions can also be annoyingly addictive and their constant misuse, emotionally harmful. At first it seems hard trying to break that which has become a habit. Overuse of what we can mistakenly call our defects of character: anger, shame, remorse and suchlike, are often part of the reason why we lose our way. As a saving grace we pander to the delusion of the false self as a mask to hide behind. Maybe this is the reason why our lives sometimes appear to be out of balance. If so, then the primary problem is nothing more than the habit of indulging the false self. Once realised, the solution becomes the exciting challenge of being part of a united recovery, allowing us to discover our authentic identity, together with the opportunity of rebuilding the reality of our true self in order to become something new, alive, unique and full of joy.

5. **Social Objectives.** Becoming established in your support group and building new relationships with its members as well as with your enablers, i.e. those whose own behaviour

allows their loved ones to continue their self-destructive patterns of behaviour

Socialising sober is, in a roundabout way, about breaking habits. With drinking and socialising there are generally two aims, which are in conflict. The first is about reaching a happy state of inebriation; the second about having an enjoyable evening with other people. However, when alcohol is involved the drinker will almost certainly lose control of both parts. By taking alcohol out of the equation it's surprising just how much enjoyment can be found in the company of others, because sober, the drinker might find themselves concentrating on the people they're with rather than on the frequency of the next drink. It's all about creating a different mindset in order to stay sober and therefore avoiding the negative consequences that excessive drinking all too often brings.

Socially, a feeling of euphoria can be set in motion before anyone even takes a drink. The very thought of a night out with your mates can cause excitement and lift a flagging mood. This has little to do with meeting your friends and a lot to do with the promise of alcohol and an excuse for taking another drink, to numb the mental stress of everyday life through achieving emotional oblivion. Attending a social event sober may feel a little uncomfortable at first but see this as a sign that you are being true to yourself and not abusing your emotions. Recognise that on a boozy evening out, it's a myth that alcohol sharpens the wit and creates enjoyable banter. It is more probable that the drinker will turn into a total nightmare when alcohol takes effect.

In recovery, make it a rule to always attend social functions in your own transport and/or have an exit strategy so that when the event ceases to be fun, you have a way out. Don't worry about saying goodbye; the cruel truth is that once your friends have had a few, they won't miss you.

Be mindful about the mental obsession: because you're on licenced premises doesn't mean you have to drink alcohol. Be precise about what you're going to drink and be assertive about it when asked. Be aware of non-alcoholic alternatives. Congratulate yourself and feel good about breaking the habit; your reward will be waking up without a hangover and not having to apologise for your behaviour the previous night.

The recovering alcoholic may still endeavour to enjoy the use of alcohol, yet at the same time attempt to stay in control of the intake. The result is always loss of control.

6. **Spiritual Objectives.** Discover and experience hope by identifying and trusting in a Higher Power, as you understand it, and by willingly acknowledging your defects of character and healing shame.

My contemporaries taught me to study the words of the AA Big Book and the 12-step programme because, like me, they believed the content to be unique to each and every one of us. By following their example I have since developed thoughts and beliefs that to some traditionalists might appear objectionable, but to me they have become the mainstay of a long, sober lifestyle. Sadly, along the way, I have witnessed many who have come through the doors of Alcoholics Anonymous and for whatever reason chosen not to stay for long enough to absorb the power of its programme. The majority, I believe, fail because their self-worth dictated that they were not worthy or even capable of success. I sometimes ask myself if the words *'God as we understood Him'* possibly turn more people away than most because the task of finding a benevolent Higher Power can appear completely hopeless to the raw newcomer.

Yet if we take a second more detailed look at step two it doesn't actually ask us to find a *'Power greater than ourselves'* it asks that we *'Came to believe that a Power greater than ourselves...'* could restore us to sanity. This shows me that step two actually assumes that the Higher Power already exists and that given time we will come to believe it can help solve our problem. Page 45 of the Big Book states quite clearly that this is what the book is about. It says, *'Its main object is to enable you to find a Power greater than yourself that will solve your problem.'* At first glance this alone appears to be a huge task, but it's not necessarily a hopeless one. Reading other literature also helped me a great deal: St Francis' prayer, for example, as written in the AA's *Twelve Steps and Twelve Traditions* informs me of the attributes of the Higher Power, being faith hope and love and so on. A little book I discovered, written by Henry Drummond over one hundred years ago and called *The Greatest Thing in the World*, analyses the first book of Corinthians chapter 13, and details a love which never fails, breaking it down into smaller enduring virtues such as patience, kindness, generosity and humility, virtues which never change with the passing of time.

Many years ago I recall my father telling me about a time when as a boy, a biplane, an aeroplane made out of wood with cotton covered wings, landed on the local football field and he and half the village turned out to see this incredible piece of engineering. I myself am old enough to remember sitting in front of a tiny black and white television set in the early hours of a cold February morning in 1964 to watch Cassius Clay beat Sonny Liston to become the world heavyweight boxing champion of the world. Nowadays, I have a small device called Alexa, not much bigger than a coffee mug, which will, if I ask it, find me a flight on a passenger jet, give me an up-to-date sports report or play me any piece of music I want to listen to, all operated from my mobile phone. In contrast, my local church operates in the same way as it has done for a thousand years, with its congregation singing hymns written hundreds of years ago. This tells me that technology, like my father's biplane and my black and white TV, fades away into little more than fond memories, but the love Henry Drummond writes about, consisting of patience, kindness, generosity, humility and so on, I have come to believe, never die.

So, step 3: *'Made a decision to turn our will and our lives over to the care of God as we understood Him'*, doesn't ask that we change our lives, it asks no more than we make a decision to change our lives in order to enjoy a long and sober lifestyle. This decision allows us to take a searching and fearless moral inventory of ourselves, seek forgiveness by making amends and put our mistakes behind us. Only then can we find the expression of God in others, and in the world around us.

A Controversy of God

'... *as we understood Him*' must mean that there was originally some debate about the issue.

I'm never quite sure what indicators or statistics professionals use to measure success in recovery. What I do know is that the fall off rate in Alcoholics Anonymous in the first three years of a member's recovery is abysmal. As a regular attendee of this otherwise steadfast support group I can only put this down to a misunderstanding of what I, all too often, hear called, *'The God thing'*. So, at the risk of being controversial, might I suggest to the atheist, agnostic or those blinded by denial, that they take another look?

The confusion can be understood if we look at what the programme says. Step 2 calls it, *'a Power greater than ourselves'*. Step 3 says, *'God as we understood Him'*, and in steps 5 and 6 it's simply, *'God'*. Step 7 is more specific – it uses the word, *'Him'*. On page 84 of the Big Book it goes further by stating that, *'Love and tolerance of others is our code.'* Similarly, John 8:32 in the Bible tells us to, *'...know the Truth and the Truth shall make you free.'* In the King James version of The Bible also claims that *'God is love'*.

Are you confused?

Instead of taking these descriptions as 'Gospel' let's see what happens if we translate this older philosophy into a more modern programme of action. For instance:

- A *'Power greater…'* could become any tangible resource outside of ourselves
- *'God as we understood Him'* would translate as the surrendering of the ego
- God could be any divine being of our choosing
- Him, a specific deity
- Love and tolerance turns into a moral code
- Love becomes patience, tolerance, understanding, etc.
- Truth is simply another word for self-honesty

Aren't we now spoiled for choice?

First, let's see what happens when we do the same thing with spirituality.

One dictionary definition is: *'Relating to or affecting the human spirit or soul'*. In programme terms this is nothing more than *an awareness of our inner conscience.* The dictionary also states that spirituality is *'A relationship based on a profound level of mental or emotional communion'*. More simply put: *the ability to honestly communicate the way we feel to another.*

Finally, the dictionary goes on to say that *'spirituality means not being concerned with material values or pursuits'*. To change this means *a significant shift in our personal primary purpose.*

My own, and I hope less complicated, definition of spirituality is: *'The continuous feeling of well-being brought about through*

the unending practice of the 12-step programme in all our affairs'.
Whatever definition you chose, it will require action! An often
missed and simple sentence at the beginning of the Big Book
Promises, clearly states, *'The spiritual life is not a theory, we have
to live it'.* In my words, practising the programme is relatively
simple – but not necessarily easy. But you do need to be willing
to try. Action therefore equates to a continuous amount of effort
and discipline and the avoidance of complacency. You must have
seen the card which reads, *'Easy does it – but do it'.*

If you are to prosper in recovery, know that you will most defi-
nitely need the help of others, and by doing so you will develop
lifelong relationships along the way. Continued positive action
results in a passion about your own recovery, allowing you to
enjoy the journey and willingly pass on what you learn, as and
when you learn it. If you do all of this then I believe spirituality
is guaranteed. Following the guidance of God does not necessarily mean following the rigid rules and instructions laid down
by the mysterious sages of the past. I find that the words of God
are more often than not the soft, warm gentle words of conscience, whispered daily in my own heart. Words that through
my journey of sobriety I have learnt to love and trust. Finally,
consider this: if God is Love, as the Bible states, then spirituality
is something we do to achieve that love, not just something we
believe in, or know or experience. Take into account the amount
of effort needed to establish the importance of a Higher Power in
your recovery and in so doing consider instead that the *essential
contributing factor* to sustained quality recovery, *is the effort itself,*
not necessarily the Higher Power.

Denial and Acceptance

**In the process of recovery denial
becomes a dangerous adversary.**

When alcoholics deny their active addiction, they risk becoming sicker. Unless they can find a genuine and honest desire to challenge it, denial becomes a totally self-defeating and self-destructive force blinding us to the reality of its impairment. Although denial can be a normal, natural, instinctive response, a defence against the painful and uncomfortable emotions that our conscious mind naturally seeks to avoid when threatened, it remains a common and recognisable symptom of active alcoholism, which, if left untreated, can keep the alcoholic in everlasting ignorance. Denial is the lie that keeps us from acknowledging the truth of our illness, therefore eliminating the possibility of positive behavior change.

Bear in mind also that the power of the alcoholic's denial runs the risk of being carried over to others such as family members and significant others, whose vulnerable minds are influenced into believing that the alcoholic's problem is due to depression or some other excusable problem, causing them to shield the alcoholic from the full consequences of their addictive behavior.

When the need to deny has been exhausted, when anger and the corrupt deals fail to impress and when sadness and depression are no longer an appropriate means of behavior, then the acceptance stage is reached. Acceptance does not mean resignation, admitting defeat or a sense of *'what's the use?'* Acceptance does not imply you are devoid of feeling, or that the conflict is over. It's not about finding balance but more about accepting the imbalance. Only with acceptance do we find that personal growth is possible. This implies that we no longer have to endure painful emotions, but are changed, improved, even enriched by the exhilarating experience of the possibility of change. However, initially, this spiritual recognition may not be readily available; again, it requires action and the need to trust in a higher power, whatever you chose that to be. Only then is it possible to accept denial and grow but initially the process may not be particularly comfortable. There could be periods of confusion, vulnerability, loneliness, and isolation in which an acute sense of powerlessness or loss of control may be experienced. Yet with practice, acceptance becomes an important part of recovery, one which requires the needed action. However, denial means we don't readily choose to accept our emotional or physical pain or difficult relationships. Managing these things constructively requires effort, which can be frustrating at first, but every time you practice acceptance you create a sense of wellbeing, which strengthens sobriety and eases the risk of future stress.

In early recovery it's important to understand and make a commitment to the acceptance process as it's both valid and beneficial, and important to your ongoing progress. Acceptance can also be practiced in our understanding of difficult people and painful emotions. For contented recovery, acceptance needs to be active in all areas of life, in all attitudes, values, beliefs and behaviors. It means recognising that the current nature of any problem can only be changed by first accepting that it's we who need to change.

The material read at the start of all AA meetings states quite clearly that the primary purpose of the recovering alcoholic is to stay sober. If we chose to deny this fact then alcohol becomes that rapacious creditor, waiting in the wings to separate us from all we hold dear.

(Reading: Acceptance was the Answer – AA Big Book, 4th **ed. p407)**

The Difficulties of Step Four

The Inventory Process

**After acknowledging that our primary
purpose is to stay sober, let us then remind
ourselves of the purpose of the 12 steps?**

1. To help us discover and establish a conscious relation-
    ship with a Power greater than ourselves.
2. To help us improve our conscious relationship with this
    Power greater than ourselves.
3. To produce the personality change necessary for our
    recovery.
4. To provide a design for living that can help us be happy,
    comfortable and at ease with ourselves, living an enjoy-
    able life of purpose, in peace and harmony with others,
    growing in understanding and effectiveness, and serving
    and being of help without the use of alcohol or other
    drugs.

The precise instructions for practicing the 12 steps are contained
in the book, *Alcoholics Anonymous* (the Big Book). The preface to
the first edition clearly states the book's purpose: *'To show other*

alcoholics precisely how we have recovered is the main purpose of this book'.

Many recovering alcoholics believe there is much more to life than being physically sober. It is true that there is much more to sobriety than just having the obsession for alcohol removed. A sober life will not be enjoyable unless we can learn to be happy and contented and sober: for a contented and sober life we require the addition of *emotional* sobriety.

The fourth step can be seen as the step which moves us forward towards physical and emotional sobriety. By taking the fourth step we are beginning the process of recreating our lives. We have already decided to give up our old plans for living and commit ourselves to the guidance of the 12-step programme. The fourth step therefore becomes the first action step. It is here that we discover if we have been thorough in steps 1, 2 and 3.

Step 4 is an analytical and fact-finding process. We are now at the stage where we need to search for causes and conditions, to uncover the truth about ourselves, both good and bad. For the sake of our ongoing recovery, we need to discover the attitudes, thoughts, beliefs, fears, actions, behaviors, and the behavior patterns, that have been blocking us, triggering problems and causing us to trip and falter, when we have an honest desire to learn the exact nature our wrongs and what caused us to do the unacceptable things we did in our inebriated past. Step 4 is also about discovering our positive assets, so that once the defects are removed, we can acquire and live with a positive mindset, positive thoughts, positive beliefs, actions, and behaviors for our highest good, and for the highest good of those with whom we come in contact. This process prepares us to live a life of purpose where we can be of maximum benefit and service to others. By taking an honest inventory and learning the exact nature of our wrongs, we will be ready to recognise when we might be slipping into our old way of life and heading for new problems, and possibly relapse.

Finally, remind yourself that step 4 is an ongoing process.

Five Negative Emotions
found in most Alcoholics

**In my experience there are five negative
emotions to watch out for, which can be
found in most addicts. They are:**

Anger

- Resentment, frustration, intolerance, etc. Or:
- Aggressive punishment, withdrawal of affection, passive-aggressive behaviour

Low self-worth

- Self-doubt, self-criticism, self-hatred, a lack of personal esteem, etc. Or:
- Abandonment issues, insecurity and anxiety

Sensitivity

- Rejection, not fitting in, a feeling of being special and/or different. Or:
- Feeling trapped in submissive co-dependent relationships

Isolation

- Self-pity, depression, *'poor me'* perspective. Or:
- Fear of retaliation, avoidance, suppression of feelings

Obsessive/compulsive behaviour

- It is the first drink that does the damage, perfectionism, OCD etc. Or:
- Unnecessary responsibility for others, the need for praise, control, the inability to do nothing

When find ourselves stuck in a state of internal dysfunction, collectively these same issues keep looping through the brain. They perpetuate the illness, help maintain the drama, ruin relationships, reinforce self-will and keep us away from God.

The question to ask yourself now is; how do you break the loop?

Letting Go Of Anger

**The saying goes:
I want what I want, and I want it now.**

Not surprisingly, we tend to want everything from recovery, immediately. For instance we want to understand others as well as ourselves, to have fellowship and to avoid loneliness, to forgive and find contentment and hope. And then when we fail to succeed we get angry.

I can offer you four ways to deal with anger.

Identify the Loss

Initially, we don't need forgiveness, or to find another perspective, or to look at the situation differently. For the first step, when dealing with anger, it's crucial that we allow time and the opportunity to identify our hurt, and experience what exactly it is we feel we have lost. It can be a relief to put into our own words what we see as our biggest losses, such as the loss of self-worth or perhaps the opportunity to have a normal healthy upbringing. But first we need to admit those losses and allow time to own them and feel them for ourselves.

Often the wounds of anger remain fresh even though we may find it hard to admit the truth. We all need time to accept our pain as real and to embrace the honesty that comes from being able to feel hurt for a while. Don't rely on denial by refusing to grieve. Avoid words such as *'I'm fine'*, *'I'm strong'*, *'I'll get over it'* – these are not an indicator of strength and are not in the least helpful.

Forgiveness

As long as we remain bitter and unforgiving of ourselves and others, we're still squeezing the sharp object in our hand and we conveniently forget that we're the ones doing the squeezing. Forgiveness doesn't mean we're condoning or justifying the bad behaviour, whether it's our own or someone else's. What forgiveness means is that we're giving up our negative dependency on it and letting go of the unreal expectation that the other person might make satisfactory amends. Instead, we need to find the resolve to untie the knot that keeps us emotionally entwined and to make that difficult decision knowing that without it we can't fully heal.

Having a recovery programme tells me that everything God does is done out of love, for our ultimate good and for an absolute purpose. So be committed to search for the gratitude hiding behind the pain. Being grateful helps us to understand what's important in life and what part of our behaviour is no longer acceptable. My fellowship colleagues tell me that the grateful alcoholic is a sober alcoholic.

Let compassion replace resentment.

Hurt people hurt people or so the saying goes.

Once we have gone through the first stages of the process of letting go of anger, we become ready to carry out the difficult but liberating task of shifting our perspective to the recognition that we generally only act badly when we feel bad. When we focus on the bad behaviour, we naturally feel resentment and self-loathing. But by looking beyond the bad behaviour, we begin to identify the hurt, emotionally scarred person beneath.

Only then can we replace resentment with true compassion.

Write a letter.

The final step in working through the process of letting go of anger is to write a letter to the person you believe hurt you the most, even if it is yourself. I'm not suggesting you send the letter. Instead, read it out to someone you trust and then destroy it. It is the writing not the sending that will set you free. We all want to be grateful for God's loving hand and the grace he bestows on us. It's our honest desire to be a loyal friend and to take pleasure in our new life, in our children and our loving families. However if we continue to experience unresolved anger, we won't be able to live out these values to the full. We'll continue to sabotage those deeper relationships with anger, criticism, negativity and withdrawal. We need to be committed and willing to take absolute responsibility for the release of our unresolved anger.

Remember, no matter what trauma you may have experienced, you have the ability to do this.

Self-esteem: our fickle foe

**God whispers in my heart while
the Devil shouts in my ear.**

It can be hard to diagnose what exactly causes low self-esteem because the things that affect our self-esteem differ for everyone. Very often difficult or stressful life experiences contribute to low self-esteem, making it one of the character traits most associated with addiction. This means that people who, for whatever reason, don't value themselves greatly are at high risk of some form of addiction. Having a pessimistic outlook, a lack of self-belief, or the inability to deal with difficult emotional issues can open the door to alcohol and drug misuse, as substances which appear to offer a solution to painful emotions. In fact, the addict is not dealing with the problem at all, rather they are merely attempting to hide from it.

The Inner Voice

Even in the most confident people, self-esteem can be fickle. For instance if someone pays us a compliment we feel good about ourselves and our self-esteem rises, if they criticise we may feel bad and it falls. Similarly our past experiences, even those we don't want to think about, are all alive and active in our daily life in the form of an **inner voice**. Although most of us won't hear this voice in the same way we would a spoken one, in many ways it acts in a similar way, constantly repeating those original negative messages to us.

For those of us with healthy self-esteem the inner voice can be positive and reassuring. However, for those with a fractured self-worth, the voice becomes a harsh judge, constantly criticising and belittling any positive accomplishments. Outwardly we might act as if all is well, while inside we feel terrified because of the belief that we are actually failures living with the fear of being found out. Alternatively we might become losers, unable to cope with the world, waiting for someone or something to come to the rescue. Either way, a case of low self-esteem can have devastating consequences.

Improving Self-esteem

To improve self-esteem, one must first believe that it can be changed. Change doesn't necessarily happen quickly or easily, it may take time but it can and does happen. We are not powerless! Once we've accepted, or have become willing to accept the possibility that we're not powerless, there are four steps we can take to begin to change our self-esteem.

- **Step 1: Challenge the inner critic.** Stop generalising unrealistically and try being reassuring and honest with yourself
- **Step 2: Find hope by renewing your inner voice**. Hold onto the belief that everything will be okay and that difficult emotions can be managed. Practise self-care and tell yourself regularly that you're a worthwhile person

51

- **Step 3: Seek help from others.** This is probably the most important phase as well as being the most difficult. Those with low self-worth have lost the ability to ask for help because they feel they don't deserve it. But as low self-esteem is often related how people treated you in the past, you may need the help of other people in the present to challenge the critical messages that come from negative past experiences.

Finally: make a written list of the following about yourself:

a)   Five things you like about your personality
b)   Five things you have achieved
c)   Five people who care about you
d)   Five things that you feel grateful for

...and then share them with another trusting person.

Submissive Co-dependent Relationships

**The risk of loving an alcoholic is
forgetting that you are special too.**

I have heard co-dependency referred to as an over-sensitive dysfunction in adulthood, which has grown from the emotional deprivation experienced in childhood. Whether this is accurate or not, this form of dysfunction often leads to unhealthy, uncontrollable relationship issues, such as addictive/compulsive behaviour as well as self-destructive and self-seeking acts of personal and family destruction. What I do know for certain is that for the over-sensitive alcoholic struggling to maintain a relationship; co-dependency can be described as an ongoing and dramatic battle of over-sensitive egos where those involved endlessly rotate between the power-seeking positions of, persecutor, rescuer and victim. Co-dependency and family dysfunction become a problem when one member relies on the other for meeting their emotional and self-esteem needs. It can also describe a problematic relationship that provides one or both parties with the means to maintain their irresponsible, addictive, or underachieving behaviour.

Chris Sharpe

The underlying addiction issues of co-dependency and dysfunction all too frequently include the misuse of drugs and alcohol. Such dysfunctional behaviour not only affects relationships, work and social life etc. but can result in physical, emotional and mental abuse. All too often family members exist in a state of, anger, pain and shame, and/or chronic mental and emotional fear, all of which may be ignored or denied through the numbing effect of alcohol, together with an unhealthy culture of finger-pointing blame.

The negative traits of co-dependent people are many and generally include an irrepressible desire for drama and an exaggerated sense of responsibility for the actions of others, resulting in an over-sensitive reaction when their efforts aren't recognised. Co-dependent traits can also involve a fear of abandonment or being alone – the co-dependent will do anything to hold on to a relationship or avoid the pain of being emotionally rejected or abandoned and they also show an extreme need for approval and recognition along with a sense of guilt when asserting themselves. Other traits include a compelling need to control others and difficulty identifying feelings

Poor boundaries and problems with assertiveness can also be found as symptoms of co-dependency. Boundaries apply not only to the self but to money, belongings, feelings, thoughts and needs. Co-dependent families often experience a detrimental responsibility for other member's feelings and problems or tend to blame their own dysfunction on someone else. Alternatively, co-dependents may develop rigid boundaries, becoming private and withdrawn, or occasionally they may waver between the two.

Being assertive is one of the many positive skills to be learnt in recovery. Through active addiction, co-dependent family members lose the ability to listen and communicate effectively with other members and in so doing, become unassertive and without boundaries. As part of the recovery process they need to learn how to communicate their needs in a concise, direct and emotionally open manner. In addition it's essential that they also become aware of others' needs as well as their own. For the recovering alcoholic, being assertive is a crucial part of improving family relationships as well as their own self-esteem.

Truth and Honesty

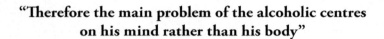

"Therefore the main problem of the alcoholic centres on his mind rather than his body"

AA big Book page 23

For whatever reason, in the practicing addict truth and honesty are two things which generally stay hidden deep within the mind for whatever reason, More often than not, what comes out of the mouth are well intentioned words designed to impress others in order to convince them that we are something that we're not. This instantly causes communication problems because in our vain attempt to impress others we do not listen to understand, what we do is listen to reply. By doing this we tend only to fool ourselves by pretending we're something that we're not. We deprive ourselves by being insincere, instead of seeking an inner freedom by not having anything to hide, thus perpetuating the illness.

For the alcoholic, being honest and open with others is not easy yet alternatively the pain of hiding the truth can be emotionally crippling. Instead, we need to remind ourselves that hearing our truth and honesty is invaluable to those with whom we share love and fellowship. In this ever changing world we need to get a firm grip on what we see and feel is genuine; we need to secure an inner calm and serenity; we need to hold on to, and believe in the true constants, such as honesty, love, fellowship and faith in a God of our understanding.

In practice, initially we should attempt to be honest with our family, close friends and our colleagues in the fellowship of Alcoholics Anonymous. We should share with them the truth about what we've been through and what we have experienced and where we are now, it is important that we avoid denying them the truth about our alcoholism. If only for the sake of our ongoing sobriety, it is essential that we spend some time with a trusted friend or colleague examining the bare essentials of truth and honesty. For instance, should we be honest enough to expose ourselves to people who might not understand? Step nine in our programme suggests that we should be honest with others except when to do so would injure or cause them harm. Ask yourself, would it be right and proper if we completely opened ourselves up and confessed our past wrongdoings to all and sundry, or on the other hand would the thing to do be to hold on to our secrets and suffer the extremes of guilt and shame. Step three suggests that we should make a decision to turn our will and our lives over to the care of a God of our understanding. So, rather than embarrass ourselves, perhaps it would be wise if we chose to pause for a moment first to ask our Higher Power to guide us and give us the needed direction and the wisdom to know the difference?

Perfectionism

In her book, *The Gifts of Imperfection*, Brené Brown states: *'Understanding the difference between healthy striving and perfectionism is critical to laying down the shield and picking up your life. Research shows that perfectionism hampers success. In fact, it's often the path to depression, anxiety, addiction, and life paralysis.'*

I see perfectionism as being a tendency to expect too much from others and from ourselves. As perfectionists we tend to idealise ourselves and the world, as well as the people in it. We set standards for ourselves and others that are impossible to attain. Consequently, too much time is spent on dwelling on the faults of others, rather than on our own imperfections. Therefore, perfectionism becomes a subtle and perverse form of self-satisfaction, which permits us to remain comfortably unaware of our own faults.

For perfectionists 'winning is everything'. However, the problem with this type of thinking or behaviour is that if we are unable to manage an emotion or a feeling by ourselves, we view it as some sort of personal defeat, which can result in anger, resentment, frustration and low self-esteem. Yet it is possible to overcome perfectionism by accepting our limitations as imperfect human beings and in this way we can learn to accept not only ourselves, but other people as well. Perfectionism is often the result of a false sense of pride or an excuse to save face. It's an egotistical condition, one that fails to surface if we focus on being of service to others rather than on ourselves.

Paradoxically, when our minds are caught up in 'self' we're unable to truly see the opportunities around us to improve our own situation and that of others. Focusing on our self-perceived inadequacies is self-serving, and until we become willing to give up the mask of perfection, we'll remain dissatisfied.

When talking about step 1, Narcotics Anonymous literature says: *'When we admit our powerlessness and inability to manage our own lives, we open the door for a Power greater than ourselves to help us. It is not where we were that counts, but where we are going.'*

Why not think of this *'Power greater'* as simply being a new way of doing things?

The Process of Change

Only through sober action can we even begin to change, grow and restore our sanity.

I have committed to memory the fact that I was told right at the beginning that recovery was all about change. When I asked what it was that needed to change, I was told quite bluntly and repeatedly that everything had to change. To make it quite clear, a tutor set out on a whiteboard the detailed extent of what it was that needed to be changed.

- Beliefs
- Behaviors
- Attitudes
- Values

Although short, this was a precise and specific list of all the personality and behavioral traits I needed to change through the practice of the 12-step programme, and I was soon to discover that these changes required action. But I was also to learn that we tend to go through several basic stages before the above required action is reached. However, be aware that it is in the nature of addiction for most people in early recovery to reject the need to change before they successfully go on to discover its importance.

The process for action set out in the DiClemente and Prochaska's Stages of Change Model, set out below.

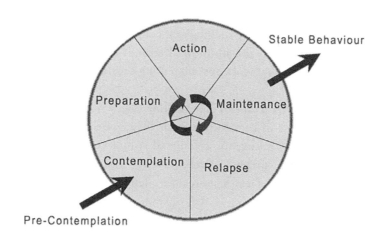

STAGES OF CHANGE MODEL

Prior to any desire to change we generally find ourselves stuck in a void called **Pre-contemplation** which means we are most likely looking for a way out, or at best we may be looking at the way forward. Please note that those in precontemplation are not intending to act or maybe demoralised from trying and failing

The next stage, usually when we attend our first AA meeting, is where we actually enter the cycle proper. This stage we call **Contemplation**, this happens though the honest sharing of others and is when we finally begin to acknowledge to ourselves that there really is a problem and maybe we need to begin to think about solving it. Be aware that contemplation may bring about anxiety which erroneously tells us there is no great rush and creates doubt and delay.

The third stage in our cycle is called **Preparation:** its here, with the help and support of the recovery fellowship that we begin to test the water by making the suggested changes to our behaviour. Preparation requires the addition of faith or belief that the programme does in fact work and the taking of small steps towards action..

Preparation leads us on to the **Action** stage where we actually start the process of transforming our beliefs, behaviour, values and attitudes by taking the calculated risk of committing ourselves to the full process of recovery. By now, we're probably staunch members of our local recovery fellowship.

Once we're committed, it's action which takes us through to the **Maintenance** stage. Maintenance or practising the principles of the programme in all our affairs is crucial and puts our personal recovery above all other issues, giving it stability and making it of primary importance.

By looking at the diagram again, it's worth pointing out here that if we become complacent and fail to maintain our sobriety, we don't go back one stage; instead we find ourselves facing the devastation of Relapse and once again back to Pre- contemplation. Be aware that there are also those who remain stuck in the Relapse stage.

Always remember that as long as we don't abuse it, the cycle of change is the only way forward and should be taken as a great opportunity to learn.

Resentment

One dictionary describes resentment as: *'a feeling of anger because you have been forced to accept something that you do not like'.*

Alcoholics Anonymous has no qualms when it names resentment as, *'the "number one" offender'* for dropping out of the recovery process. It goes on to clearly state that: *'It destroys more alcoholics than anything else. From it stem all forms of spiritual disease, for we have been not only mentally and physically ill, we have been spiritually sick.'* Adding that, *'a life which includes deep resentment leads only to futility and unhappiness. To the precise extent that we permit these, do we squander the hours that might have been worthwhile.'*

I don't know about you but I find these to be scary words.

In my experience with alcoholics, resentment can be a relatively common emotion resulting in feelings of annoyance and shame, which inevitably lead to relapse. There is nothing positive about having resentments; they are painfully negative feelings which, insanely, we tend to hold on to. Even though they hurt and cut us deeply, it seems impossible to let them go. One theory is that we hold on to them so that at some time in the future we may be able hurl them back at the people who hurt us. Sadly, by doing so, we tend to end up hurting ourselves. In other words, feeding our resentment only serves to deepen our emotional wound.

Unfortunately, life is such that we all get hurt sometimes by the words or actions of others and the hurt can be easily justified. What is more difficult to justify is our inability to disengage ourselves from the event, meaning we continue to experience the pain of it long after it is done. We can attempt to drown our self-pity in alcohol but all that does is prolong the anger and frustration, poisoning our lives with bitterness and spite. Resentment creates an initial feeling of drama; we feel hard done by and have an almost insatiable urge to defend ourselves. Then the drama turns against us and we have no idea how to deal with the resulting resentment, nothing seems to work. Finally, the resentment becomes a part of who we are as a person, in as much as we become resentful people rather than someone who just shows resentful behaviour. If you think about it there is a significant difference between the two.

So how can we stop resentment from controlling our thoughts and emotions, and so achieve some inner peace? This can be more difficult than forgiving those who hurt us in the first place. However, as an alternative we could try to bring forgiveness into our own lives by forgiving ourselves and attempting to see things from a new and different perspective. Self-forgiveness or self-compassion is an important and powerful process. It allows the reality of now to push away the negative emotions of the past so we can be free of the continuing hurt and have a chance of managing frustration and anger in a more positive way.

Here are a few suggestions to help you manage resentment:

1. **Stay in the present**: When you find yourself thinking about how you were wronged yesterday, try bringing yourself back to today.
2. **Change your strategy:** Instead of focusing on what's wrong in your life, bring to mind those things which are good and positive.
3. **Stop trying to score points. Count your blessings:** The idea is not to take revenge but to achieve peace of mind and a state of contentment.
4. **Share your troubles with someone else:** Talking honestly to another understanding person brings about a spiritual shift and helps you to see things in a new and more positive light.

One sponsorship guide to the 12-step programme suggests that resentment can be thought of as you taking the poison and waiting for the other person to die.

Sober but Stuck: the Dry Drunk Syndrome

We cannot deny reality nor wish it to be different; we can only accept it and make the necessary changes.

The expression, dry drunk is an ambiguous term often used by 12-step fellowships to describe someone who no longer drinks but continues to behave in a dysfunctional way. In other words, a dry drunk is someone who has given up alcohol or drugs, but as yet has failed to make any significant emotional or behavioural changes and therefore remains stuck in the initial stages of contemplation.

The person behaving as the dry drunk is most probably not an active member of the sobriety community; therefore they fail to recognise sober realism or the true sense of sober living in their peers. As a result, their mental and emotional lives become chaotic, their approach to everyday living is unrealistic, and their behaviour, both verbal and physical, is often viewed as unacceptable.

A dry drunk is an alcoholic or addict who shows little or no outwardly sincere interest in the true nature of recovery. They may currently be abstinent but will be making little or no spiritual progress. For instance, the dry drunk could be someone who doesn't have an active sponsor, fails to adjust their lives to the guidance of a 12-step programme and whose attendance at meetings is either minimal or non-existent. As a result they may be distancing themselves from the recovery process, remaining in a negative state of mind and generally feeling ill at ease with life.

Self-esteem issues are usually found to be at the core of most addicts. Yet in the dry drunk these may be cleverly disguised by a mask of grandiosity and a sense of their own self-importance. Alternatively, their insecurity and a lack of self-worth causes them to become the resentful victim of life's misfortune. Either way, the dry drunk will become isolated and distant from friends, family and fellowship members and unable to form satisfactory relationships with those who genuinely care.

Conditions of grandiosity, being judgmental, intolerance, impulsivity and indecisiveness are recognised symptoms of Dry Drunk Syndrome. Taken separately or together, these issues can lead to mood swings, the cause of which might be wrongly blamed on others and therefore seem unrelated to the true trigger circumstances. As a result the dry drunk experiences limitations to growth, an inability to mature and fails to benefit from the possibilities that life generally offers.

By denying these shortcomings in themselves, dry drunks will often attempt to escape notice by highlighting the transgressions of others. To confuse matters even more, some alcoholics who experience Dry Drunk Syndrome may be seen as knowing all the answers, and being seldom lost for words when it comes to self-diagnosis. Their knowledge can be quite impressive and convincing.

Someone suffering from Dry Drunk Syndrome may be difficult to be around and may often seem dissatisfied with life. Their actions and attitudes might be as unpleasant as when they were actively drinking. Mood swings may come on suddenly, making the individual unpredictable and emotionally unstable. Overwhelming feelings of depression may descend without any reason followed by excited bouts of agitation, irritability or anxiety. These, plus conflicting displays of superiority or grandiosity are all unfortunate signs of Dry Drunk Syndrome.

Because we are all different and may have our own experiences with Dry Drunk Syndrome, additional signs and symptoms may include some of the following:

- Poor quality of sleep and a general feeling of negativity
- Envy and feelings of resentment towards unsuspecting friends and associates who appear able to drink normally
- Being easily overwhelmed by stress and stressful situations
- Confused emotions, impatience and the inability to concentrate or think clearly
- A longing for the excitement and drama of the old drinking days
- Boredom, complacency and the failure to maintain a positive state of mind

Some of the most effective ways in which we can cope with Dry Drunk Syndrome and thus avoid that eventual relapse include the following:

- Taking part in individual therapy or the group process by attending 12-step meetings on a regular basis

- It is also important for the Dry Drunk to make sure that expectations regarding their own recovery are realistic. Genuine encouragement from family and friends can be central to the recovery process, together with sharing successes and achievements with them
- Regular exercise and healthy eating are also crucial, as well as finding and acquiring an enjoyable hobby or learning a new skill or developing an existing talent in order to stimulate the mind
- It's important to find time to relax, or simply learn to do nothing other than be content with yourself
- Seeking help from others is crucial to the ego deflation process, along with a positive involvement in the principles of the recovery program and an honest desire to repair the wrongs done to others

Reaching out for help is hard but not as hard as not taking that first step.

Altruism and Addiction

There is a paradox in AA which states that in order to keep what we have, we have to give it away.

For the willing alcoholic who is prepared to tread the pathway to recovery it is worth mentioning here that the pathway can be paved with the odd risk or two. In this instance I need to mention altruism. Altruism is not a topic that is often discussed in recovery rooms, possibly because it's a psychological concept difficult to understand. One definition is that true altruism refers to *the unselfish concern or regard for the well-being of others without the expectation of reward*, in simple terms, unselfishly carrying the message to others. Genuine altruism can be as important to the recipient as it is to the messenger. The concept of altruism, or unselfishly carrying the message, has been crucial in the growth and success of many support fellowships since their conception, the reason being, because it works.

The true benefits of altruism in recovery are self-evident. However, the potentially damaging features of altruism have been generally overlooked or ignored completely. In our fellowship meeting we may often hear the phrase, *'ours is a selfish programme'* and such selfishness in the addict can easily turn toxic when corrupted by an out-of-control ego. One prime example of this is where the messenger feels the need to use altruistic behaviour primarily as a way to convince other people that they, the messenger, are a good and well-meaning person, a process where benevolence becomes associated with some sort of emotional trade-off used to protect the messenger's hidden hoard of guilt and shame. This process can be interpreted as an obsessive and irrational form of altruism, where attempts to promote the welfare of others risk unanticipated harm to one or both parties.

Altruism and Egotism

In the early stages of recovery, because of the painful nature of raw and untreated negative emotions, it is not unknown for alcoholics to be subconsciously pushed on by self-interest, making it difficult to prove that some form of egocentricity isn't involved in our altruistic behaviour. However, even though we may have mixed motives for our actions, it doesn't necessarily mean that those actions are not valid and that on a conscious level our altruistic intentions are not genuine. It's just that the emotions involved in our actions may become more complicated and difficult to manage, and be found unconvincing by others.

As previously stated, the long-standing and well proven paradox of Alcoholics Anonymous is: *'In order to keep what we have, we have to give it away'* which indicates that members receive benefit and a sense of well-being if they offer service to the cause. This is again borne out in the fifth tradition which clearly states: *'Each group has but one primary purpose – to carry its message to the alcoholic who still suffers.'*

Well-meaning intentions

Some people have a natural desire to help others without having to first consider the practical results of their help. However, alcoholics new to recovery may lack the needed wisdom and can be unskilled in the ways of true altruism. They may not understand how to give love without expecting something in return. Often on the instruction of a well-meaning sponsor, they may genuinely engage in what they see as true and honest altruism, yet in so doing, risk causing harm to others and themselves when their outwardly good intentions become distorted into potentially damaging ways. This form of pathological altruism has been described as *'the willingness of a person to irrationally place another's perceived needs above his or her own in a way that causes self-harm'.* Meaning, their good intentions with regard to helping others can be greatly misunderstood. I'd suggest that a way forward from this confusing dilemma is that altruistic intentions be considered first. The primary purpose of Alcoholics Anonymous is to carry its message, however, the best way of doing this may not be as immediately obvious as we initially believe, nor does it come close to that which is promoted by those more experienced in the art of recovery. In the early days, a well-used guide to our future conduct could be the Serenity Prayer, which in its final line asks us to find, *'wisdom to know the difference',* and it has been my experience that wisdom generally comes with time. My own contribution is as some wiser person once said: *'In the first instance it is better to remain silent at the risk of being thought an interfering fool, than to open your mouth and remove all doubt of it.'*

Grandiosity, the Arch-enemy of Sobriety

Grandiosity hides the joy of true success.

As previously mentioned, it is my experience and belief that low self-esteem stands at the core of active addiction, indicating that, initially, the addict has very little self-belief in their ability to be successful in recovery. This fact is often reinforced by the erroneous opinion that they are not worthy of a better, sober way of life. As a way of combating low self-esteem some alcoholics may experience periods of grandiosity. In contradiction to low self-esteem, this where they believe and act as if they are better than everyone else. An AA adage which illustrates this says, *'The alcoholic is someone who lies in the gutter looking down on others.'*

There are extremes to grandiosity: those who openly exhibit grandiosity may simply suffer from an unrealistic sense of their own importance, appearing pompous and pretentious to the observer. They may have feelings of superiority, believing nothing bad can happen to them. In severe cases the delusions of grandeur go as far as convincing the alcoholic that they really are special and different. By its very nature, grandiosity can be a difficult obstacle to overcome, mainly because it prevents the addict from finding the needed honesty and humility which is necessary to achieve successful sobriety. Accepting help becomes almost impossible, preventing the addict from gaining a true understanding of their problem. Even those with appreciative periods of sobriety may not escape the ravages of grandiosity because of the dominant belief that they are indeed a special case. They go on to reject the resources freely available to them in recovery and refuse to believe the simple philosophy that if recovery works for others then it can also work for them. They may fail to discover the qualities of a satisfying and sober life and be condemned to live the life of a dry drunk, greatly increasing the risk of relapse. However, the self-aware and willing alcoholic can combat grandiosity in a number of ways, mainly by developing humility and understanding. It is important to know that these blessings are a sign of strength and not weakness and do not appear magically overnight but require constant action. Another way of combating grandiosity is to challenge thoughts that arise about being superior to other people. This challenge can be reinforced by spending time with inspirational people in recovery who show natural humility. Again, the AA states the obvious when it says, *'Stick with the Winners.'*

Meditation such as mindfulness can also be helpful, as is keeping a daily journal reflecting on your behaviour during the day, or practising step 10 in the evening. Ask a family or fellowship member you can trust to give you feedback on your behaviour, *providing* you feel strong enough to deal with any constructive criticism arising from that. Developing self-compassion to combat the rigours of guilt and shame and a burgeoning ego is also important, as is regular attendance at recovery meetings and practising the 12-step programme with a sponsor. Above all, it's crucial not to pick up the first drink.

Finally, remember that grandiosity is the arch-enemy of successful sobriety, so don't allow it to sabotage your recovery. Start valuing yourself more highly and don't settle for anything less than the happiness and contentment that you deserve.

Shame and Guilt

'Shame, blame, disrespect, betrayal, and the withholding of affection damage the roots from which love grows. Love can only survive these injuries if they are acknowledged, healed and rare.'

Brené Brown: *The Gifts of Imperfection*

Shame and guilt are related emotions although there are notable differences between the two. Guilt is when you feel bad about something you've done, while shame goes a little deeper than guilt. Shame is the painful feeling that it is we ourselves who are flawed and in some way not worthy. With the recovering addict, shame is a primary affect; a disruptive belief that there is something very wrong with who we are, which can be severely impacted by lesser negative feelings

Below are some examples of beliefs and behaviours that might impact our shame:

- Calling a friend and when they don't call back immediately, wondering if they're angry with you about something (rejection)

- Being physically different: too fat, too thin, too tall, too short or the wrong colour (not fitting in or perceived inadequacy)
- Wanting to appear favourable to others but believing you're incapable of being so (perfectionism)
- Covering your faults with a lie and being found out (lies and deceit)
- The erroneous belief that everything is your fault (guilt)
- Uncontrollable outbursts of emotion (rage)
- Being judgemental of peers (criticism)
- Testing yourself in dangerous or risky situations (fear and self-doubt)

Being able to recognise the difference between shame and guilt is important when it comes to correcting our mistakes. We can apologise for guilt, or make amends for our wrongdoing. Shame, on the other hand, brings about actions that are self-destructive, and thoughts which are negative and self-deprecating, together with an all-consuming pain which is extremely hard to deal with. Shame is the pain and it appears that we can't escape the pain, instead we must learn how to 'suffer' all that life offers.

Yet, contrary to this, the progressive act of recovery tells me that we can also learn something positive from everything we encounter in life. If this is so, what can we learn from the pain of shame? If, as physics states, for every action, there is an equal and opposite reaction, I need to ask what could be the opposite of shame?

One dictionary definition describes compassion as: '*A deep awareness of the suffering of others coupled with the wish to relieve it.*' Whereas self-compassion is about extending compassion to oneself in instances of perceived inadequacy, failure, or general emotional suffering. This means that, rather than attempting to ignore our pain or exaggerating it, we face it by holding onto the discomfort of our negative emotions in a secure and supportive awareness. However, like other emotions in recovery, to have self-compassion you must first be aware that you're suffering. In *Hamlet*, William Shakespeare coined the phrase, '*To Thine Own Self Be True*', often borrowed by Alcoholics Anonymous. This means you can lie and deceive, say little half-truths to anyone, including yourself, but to be free from shame you need to be true to yourself. Being true to others will follow in time. If you are emotionally deceived about whom you are, shame is bound to come to the fore and you may continue to struggle. Become aware of whom you are... faults, vices, good points, strengths, weaknesses and all. The hard part of recovery is not just discovering the negative emotions but having the courage to understand and manage them!

Brené Brown says, '*If we can share our story with someone who responds with empathy and understanding, shame can't survive.*' To aid this statement, here is a simple formula that might help us to be mindful and to feel the negative pain:

- Sit with it, talk about it, and share it with others
- Name it, own it, bring it out into the open, and make it your own
- Then find self-compassion. Identify the opposed, remedial emotion, the antidote, and the contrary
- Begin to practise this in all your affairs

But I would ask you to be aware, this process could take time.

Being Special and Different

Whether recovery is sought through a treatment
centre, specialised counselling or through one
of the many worldwide recovery fellowships,
it is worth taking a moment to consider that
those who struggle and fall, are usually those
who primarily doubt their ability to achieve.

Deep down inside, most addicts are born doubters: not only
do they doubt their ability to achieve, but they also doubt their
value, and their ability to love or be loved, to the point where
they become so damaged that when they are offered restitution,
they deny it and push the opportunity away. This is mainly because they don't believe they deserve it. For the suffering addict,
achievements don't necessarily erase shame or low self-worth,
instead what he or she tends to do is mask genuine triumph with
grandiosity, false pride and an inflated ego, while allowing the
negatives of resentment and blaming others to come to the fore.
Amazingly, the 12-step programme recognises this process. It
reveals that only restitution: the forgiving of oneself and others,
compassion, repentance and living with dignity will ever erase
the pain of the past. The problem is that when the alcoholic
is faced with what seem like such terrible imperfections, then

compassion, whether for the self or for others, can seem an impossible task.

I sometimes think that in support fellowships such as AA, membership can be divided into two definite camps: both of them valid and acceptable. The first camp is for those who manage to 'keep it simple' by following the suggestions and opinions of others without question. The second camp is for members who sometimes complicate matters, finding a need to question and analyse. I believe that, in this second camp, most members find it difficult to share the unquestioning faith and conviction seen in others. Shared faith therefore becomes something of an illusion, giving a feeling of being less than, or not belonging. For this reason the comfort and conformity of a recovery fellowship can only go so far and doubting members may find themselves well and truly ensconced in the 'more complicated' camp. Playing the game doesn't seem to live up to its promise.

As opposed to relapse, further investigation into the complicated nature of addiction can become an alternative route into recovery. Despite what some sceptics may say, analysis can be a preferred option. It only becomes problematic when it blocks and obstructs progress. To survive the complication, positive effort is required. For this reason I offer up a challenge to those who question and doubt. Stick with it, not only accept the doubt but use it, push it forward to open up an essential pathway to faith. On the face of it this process may sound unconventional but I truly believe doubt can become a gateway to the positive. If challenged correctly, doubt can inspire a person to set his or her own individual goals, to draw up inspirational action plans, to seek more information, find new alternatives and discover the key that opens the door to a workable faith.

It has been said before that doubt and faith are two sides of the same coin and recovery literature tells us that, *'Faith without works is dead.'* For that reason alone, we sometimes need to just sit quietly and listen to the rationale of doubt and examine the bigger picture. The least this can do is broaden our perspective. If given half a chance, doubt can become a powerful motivator. Who knows, it may even supply you with the motivation to stay sober. Achieving a seemingly unattainable goal by proving someone, even yourself wrong by rising above the obstacle, can produce the sweet and rewarding feelings that makes a little self-doubt worthwhile. If looked at with a positive frame of mind, doubt can be transformed into the most important faith of all. Doubt invigorates faith, demands more of it, and causes us to ask more of each other. When communicated properly, doubt has the ability to bind one person's faith to another's. It encourages us to reach out, discover and explore.

Someone who doubts can be someone who firmly remains on a journey.

Depression

Depression can be described as being a state of extreme dejection or morbidly excessive melancholy, a state of hopelessness and a feeling of inadequacy, often with added physical symptoms.

Over the years I've lost count of the number of clients who began treatment by insisting that their problem was more about depression and not necessarily alcoholism, despite the fact that alcohol is a depressant. My set response is always to suggest that we first deal with the alcohol and if the depression persists we can attempt to deal with that afterwards. Surprisingly in most cases, once the alcohol was removed, the depression was soon forgotten.

Depression, like alcoholism, has a range of complex symptoms including feelings of being fed up, weary, a sense of loss, feeling useless, unloved or sad. Self-harming, self-reproach, anger, guilt and shame, the inability to concentrate and the risk of suicidal tendencies can also be painful signs. For most of us, these symptoms vary in combination, duration and how often they occur. Depression, like alcoholism, gives the sufferer a particular feeling of isolation which prevents them from seeking and accepting comfort from others. It provides a convenient wall of isolation.

There is debate as to whether a physical chemical imbalance causes depression or the depressed mood causes the physical disturbance. It's possible that depression is caused by an ongoing interaction of social, physical and psychological pressures creating a downward spiral. However, because alcoholism does obviously fit into the normal parameters of what many think of as disease, the debate continues as to whether alcoholism can be seen as being a self-induced moral failing or an incurable disease. A minority of drinkers, for example, make the decision to stop without needing much support. In counselling and psychological terms, there is general agreement that depression occurs when we start believing we're not good enough. The same applies to alcoholism. The more unacceptable we believe ourselves to be, the more drastic action we have to take to alleviate the problem.

Most counselling approaches recognise this negative lack of self-worth as key, in as much as a sense of failure to satisfy high expectations causes both alcoholism and depression. Because alcohol is a central nervous system depressant, its use tends to trigger depressive symptoms such as lethargy, sadness and hopelessness. However, many depressed individuals reach for drugs or alcohol as a way to lift their spirits or to numb painful thoughts. As a result, depression and substance abuse tend to feed into each other, where one condition will often make the other worse.

Fear of Intimacy

**Fear of intimacy is an often subconscious fear
of closeness that frequently affects our personal
relationships. During active alcoholism this fear of
physical and/or emotional intimacy tends to present
itself in the closest and most meaningful relationships.**

While there may be times when we are aware of actually being
apprehensive of and distrusting of love, we are more likely to
identify these fears as concern over potentially negative outcomes
such as rejection, the deterioration of a relationship or feelings
of affection that may not be returned, all of which tend to be
numbed by an excessive input of alcohol. Therefore, it's not
surprising to learn that the real resistance to intimacy doesn't
always come from our partner's behaviour, but from a lurking
enemy deep within us.

The problem is that the positive way a partner sees us often con-
flicts with the negative ways we have learnt to view ourselves.
Holding on to our negative self-attitudes renders us resistant to
being seen differently. Because it's difficult for us to allow the
reality of being loved to affect our basic image of ourselves, we
often build up resistance to love. These negative core beliefs are
often based on deep-seated feelings developed in early childhood,

which tell us we are essentially bad, unlovable or deficient. While these attitudes may be painful or unpleasant, at the same time they are familiar to us, and we're used to them lingering in our subconscious. As adults, we mistakenly assume that these beliefs are a fundamental flaw and are therefore impossible to correct. However, we don't intentionally reject love to preserve this familiar identity. Instead, during times of closeness and intimacy, we react with behaviours that create tension in the relationship, serving to push our loved one away.

Here are just some of the ways we distance ourselves emotionally as a result of a fear of intimacy:

- Withholding affection
- Reacting indifferently or adversely to affection or positive acknowledgement
- Becoming paranoid or suspicious of a partner
- Losing interest in one's sexuality
- Being overly critical of a partner
- Feeling guarded or resistant to being close

In our recovery, if we wish to overcome these fears of intimacy, we must challenge our negative attitudes toward ourselves and not push our loved ones away. We must attempt to challenge our core resistance to love, confront our negative self-image and nurture our tolerance for a loving relationship. Active addiction makes love not only hard to find, but strange as it may seem, even more difficult to accept and tolerate. We may declare the need for a loving partner, but many of us have deep-seated fears of intimacy that make it difficult for us to take part in a close relationship. The experience of real love tends to threaten our self-defensive denial and raises anxiety as we become vulnerable by opening ourselves up to another person. Falling in love not only brings excitement and fulfilment, it can also create anxiety, and fear of rejection and potential loss, giving the alcoholic good reason to anaesthetise their feelings. As a result we may even begin to rely on fantasy gratification rather actual interactions with other people; unlike people, fantasies can't hurt us.

Over time, we may prefer these fantasies over actual personal interactions and real positive acknowledgment or affection, making us reluctant to take another chance on being loved. As a coping mechanism, we learn not to rely on others, believing it impossible that someone could actually love and value us. These negative feelings have become a deeply embedded part of who we think we are. Therefore, when someone loves and reacts positively toward us, we experience a conflict within ourselves. We don't know whether to believe this new person's kind and loving point of view of us. So, we react with suspicion and distrust because our fear of intimacy has once again been aroused.

In the alcoholic, even though the fear of intimacy is a largely unconscious process, it can still be seen affecting the behaviour. When we push our partner away emotionally, or retreat from their affection, we're acting on this fear of intimacy by holding back the positive qualities that our partner finds most desirable. We often try to make ourselves less lovable, so we don't have to be as afraid of being loved. This display of distancing behaviour may reduce the anxiety about being too close to someone, but it comes at a great cost.

Acting on our fears preserves the negative self-image and keeps us from experiencing the great pleasure and joy that love can bring. In recovery, the fear of intimacy can be overcome. Confidence and self-worth can be developed to such a point that we cease to be afraid of love and let someone in. We start to recognise the behaviours that are driven by our fear of intimacy and challenge them. It becomes possible to remain vulnerable in relationships by resisting retreating into a fantasy of love or engaging in distancing and withholding behaviours. We can learn to maintain our integrity and gradually increase our tolerance for being loved. By taking the sober actions necessary to challenge our fear of intimacy, we can expand our capacity for both giving and accepting love.

Wellbeing and Hope

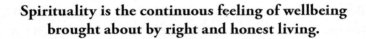

Spirituality is the continuous feeling of wellbeing brought about by right and honest living.

There is little doubt in my mind that the commonly used term, 'Spirituality or Spiritual Programme' can be extremely off-putting when delivered to the recovering addict early on in the therapy programme, yet if time is taken to define and tailor it correctly, spirituality can and should become the mainstay of any continued, quality, recovery plan. In today's difficult and challenging times, wouldn't it be good to live an incredible life full of hope, energy, joy and promise, leading to what I call well-being. But how do we find such hope, and once found how do we hold on to it? It becomes one of the many tasks of the therapist or sponsor to assist the newly recovering addict in finding the emotional strength to believe that they *can* make a difference, by enduring through difficult times.

There are many strategies available to encourage the inexperienced alcoholic to seek that illusive state of wellbeing, strategies such as restoring hope. It's so easy to lose hope during the initial days of recovery when everything is seen in a new and unfamiliar light, or when you've had a bad day and feel emotionally lost or lonely and without any real sense of progress. I believe hope can initially be found by accepting that the odd step backwards is part of life, while at the same time continuing to move forward by believing that things will always get better. The evidence is that they generally do. Hope comes by keeping an honest focus on your own recovery and by not allowing allow yourself to overlook the true joy that sobriety can bring, even when the people around you seem to be stuck in their own negativity. Try not to lose perspective. A bad day sober is always better than a good day drunk!

Another strategy is to determine positive and achievable goals by putting them down in a plan. An alcoholic in early recovery will certainly lose hope if they have no plan. Plans must always be flexible, your goals need to be something you can work towards but change or alter if required, because at times throughout your ongoing sobriety, you will uncover new thoughts or actions which may make it easier to direct your focus in achieving your plan. In turn, achievement brings hope and we deserve hope as much as we deserve to have dreams. So even when times are not so good, never give up on your dreams. Tell yourself often that you deserve them.

Given time and the right sort of guidance, these basic strategies will go on to form the principles of this new and exciting life that I chose to call wellbeing. It does exist and it's available to those who are prepared to accept the help and put in the right action. Why don't you give it a try?

Emotional Sobriety:
The Next Frontier

The following article was written by Bill W. and published in the AA Grapevine in January 1958.

I think that many oldsters who have put our AA "booze cure" to severe but successful tests still find they often lack emotional sobriety. Perhaps they will be the spearhead for the next major development in AA—the development of much more real maturity and balance (which is to say, humility) in our relations with ourselves, with our fellows, and with God.

Those adolescent urges that so many of us have for top approval, perfect security, and perfect romance—urges quite appropriate to age seventeen—prove to be an impossible way of life when we are at age forty-seven or fifty-seven.

Since AA began, I've taken immense wallops in all these areas because of my failure to grow up, emotionally and spiritually. My God, how painful it is to keep demanding the impossible, and how very painful to discover finally, that all along we have had the cart before the horse! Then comes the final agony of seeing how awfully wrong we have been, but still finding ourselves unable to get off the emotional merry-go-round.

How to translate a right mental conviction into a right emotional result, and so into easy, happy, and good living—well, that's not only the neurotic's problem, it's the problem of life itself for all of us who have got to the point of real willingness to hew to right principles in all our affairs.

Even then, as we hew away, peace and joy may still elude us. That's the place so many of us AA oldsters have come to. And it's a hell of a spot, literally. How shall our unconscious—from which so many of our fears, compulsions and phony aspirations still stream—be brought into line with what we actually believe, know and want! How to convince our dumb, raging and hidden "Mr. Hyde" becomes our main task.

I've recently come to believe that this can be achieved. I believe so because I begin to see many benighted ones — folks like you and me – commencing to get results. Last autumn [several years back – ed.] depression, having no really rational cause at all, almost took me to the cleaners. I began to be scared that I was in for another long chronic spell. Considering the grief I've had with depressions, it wasn't a bright prospect.

I kept asking myself, "Why can't the Twelve Steps work to release depression?" By the hour, I stared at the St. Francis Prayer…"It's better to comfort than to be the comforted." Here was the formula, all right. But why didn't it work?

Suddenly I realized what the matter was. My basic flaw had always been dependence – almost absolute dependence – on people or circumstances to supply me with prestige, security, and the like. Failing to get these things according to my perfectionist dreams and specifications, I had fought for them. And when defeat came, so did my depression–

There wasn't a chance of making the outgoing love of St. Francis a workable and joyous way of life until these fatal and almost absolute dependencies were cut away.

Because I had over the years undergone a little spiritual development, the absolute quality of these frightful dependencies had never before been so starkly revealed. Reinforced by what Grace I could secure in prayer, I found I had to exert every ounce of will and action to cut off these faulty emotional dependencies upon people, upon AA, indeed, upon any set of circumstances whatsoever.

Then only could I be free to love as Francis had. Emotional and instinctual satisfactions, I saw, were really the extra dividends of having love, offering love, and expressing a love appropriate to each relation of life.

Plainly, I could not avail myself of God's love until I was able to offer it back to Him by loving others as He would have me. And I couldn't possibly do that so long as I was victimized by false dependencies.

For my dependency meant demand—a demand for the possession and control of the people and the conditions surrounding me.

While those words "absolute demand" may look like a gimmick, they were the ones that helped to trigger my release into my present degree of stability and quietness of mind, qualities which I am now trying to consolidate by offering love to others regardless of the return to me.

This seems to be the primary healing circuit: an outgoing love of God's creation and His people, by means of which we avail ourselves of His love for us. It is most clear that the current can't flow until our paralyzing dependencies are broken, and broken at depth. Only then can we possibly have a glimmer of what adult love really is.

Spiritual calculus, you say? Not a bit of it. Watch any AA of six months working with a new Twelfth Step case. If the case says "To the devil with you," the Twelfth Stepper only smiles and turns to another case. He doesn't feel frustrated or rejected. If his next case responds, and in turn starts to give love and attention to other alcoholics, yet gives none back to him, the sponsor is happy about it anyway. He still doesn't feel rejected; instead he rejoices that his one-time prospect is sober and happy. And if his next following case turns out in later time to be his best friend (or romance) then the sponsor is most joyful. But he well knows that his happiness is a by-product—the extra dividend of giving without any demand for a return.

The really stabilizing thing for him was having and offering love to that strange drunk on his doorstep. That was Francis at work, powerful and practical, minus dependency and minus demand.

In the first six months of my own sobriety, I worked hard with many alcoholics. Not a one responded. Yet this work kept me sober. It wasn't a question of those alcoholics giving me anything. My stability came out of trying to give, not out of demanding that I receive.

Thus I think it can work out with emotional sobriety. If we examine every disturbance we have, great or small, we will find at the root of it some unhealthy dependency and its consequent unhealthy demand. Let us, with God's help, continually surrender these hobbling demands. Then we can be set free to live and love; we may then be able to Twelfth Step ourselves and others into emotional sobriety.

Of course I haven't offered you a really new idea—only a gimmick that has started to unhook several of my own "hexes" at depth. Nowadays my brain no longer races compulsively in either elation, grandiosity or depression. I have been given a quiet place in bright sunshine.

Sponsorship

Only through the process of honest identification with another caring human being can we rediscover our lost self-worth.

Any wise sage in a recovery fellowship will gladly tell you that recovery from addiction cannot possibly be done on your own, which is the whole point of having a fellowship. However, within the confines of that group association, individual advice and support is also required and we call this sponsorship. So, what exactly does sponsorship mean?

As mentioned earlier, there is a unique 12-step paradox which states: *'In order to keep what we have we have to give it away.'* What this generally means is that someone with a reasonable extent of sobriety, who becomes a mentor to the newcomer by sharing what he or she has learnt, will miraculously discover that, through the sharing, both their sober lives will be improved beyond measure. The newcomer, when first attending fellowship meetings, may initially feel confused and hesitant and will have many questions. Although regular members will always be willing to respond, closer, more informal support may be needed in coming to terms with the complexities of living a sober life. So it's suggested that the newcomer selects a member with whom they feel comfortable and relaxed, and to whom they can talk freely and confidentially, and asks that person to be their sponsor.

If you feel ready and in need of a sponsor then don't delay. It's important to find someone from the recovery fellowship with whom you identify.

In choosing please consider the following suggestions:

- A sponsor should always be the same gender
- A sponsor should have at least two years of continuous sobriety or clean-time and have a good working knowledge of the 12-step programme
- A sponsor should be sponsored themselves
- A sponsor should be readily available and easily contactable
- Ultimately, a sponsor should become a sympathetic friend
- It may also be helpful if a sponsor has a similar background and interests to the person they sponsor.

Some things to consider in the sponsor's role:

- The sponsor should emphasise that it is the recovery programme which holds primary importance in the relationship
- A sponsor must be committed within the limits of personal experience and programme knowledge to helping the newcomer to stay sober
- A sponsor must lead by example
- A good sponsor regularly attends meetings and also encourages his sponsee to attend a variety of meetings
- A sponsor should be accepting, non-judgemental and demonstrate an open mind

- Sponsors should never try to impose their personal views on the sponsee
- A sponsor must be sometimes willing to admit they don't know. Nor should they pretend to know all the answers

Our primary purpose is to stay sober and carry the message…

As recovering addicts we can't afford to lose sight of the importance of sponsorship. Experience shows that the newcomer who desires to find contented recovery and get the most out of their recovery programme should not hesitate in seeking a sponsor's help and guidance.

Sponsorship is a priority and too important to be left to chance.

Most current members of Alcoholics Anonymous owe their sobriety to the fact that someone else took a special interest in them and was willing to share the gift of sobriety.

The best way to get a sponsor is to ask!

...And Now

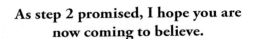

**As step 2 promised, I hope you are
now coming to believe.**

In the beginning some of us asked ourselves what we then believed to be a valid question: 'If there is a God in this life then
why did he inflict us with this dreadful illness?' The answer
now is obvious; so that we would have to ask Him to help us to
recover from it, for when we look back that is the truth of what
happened. Yet in the busy-ness of our day, we can sometimes
forget to stop and thank Him for all that is good in our lives as a
result of our seeking His help. Today we are free from the burden
of alcohol and our blessings are many, and when we do recall
God's part in our emotional good fortune, our heart fills with
gratefulness for the gift of living, for the ability to love and be
loved in return, for the opportunity to see the everyday wonders
of creation, for sleep and awakening and for a mind that thinks
clearly and a body that is able to experience true emotion.

It takes a long time of working hard at sobriety to discover what
God, as we understood Him, was for us. Then, in a protracted
moment of spiritual enlightenment, we realised that God was
love, nothing more and nothing less and that his love was what
we had to give to others. This notion was something at which
we initially baulked. Up until that moment we had never found

the need to consider what love really meant. All our lives we had taken for granted that love was something that others had to give to us. This new concept caused much thought and consternation and yet it felt right.

So the question we have to ask today is have we even come even close to achieving emotional sobriety? Have we been able to develop spiritually? Have we been able to avail ourselves of God's love and offer it back to others? One would certainly hope so, yet when the serenity of a peaceful weekend wears off, usually by the following Monday afternoon and life takes over, where is love then? In Bill Wilson's article, which we looked at earlier, he openly acknowledges that, *'he had come to believe that this (emotional sobriety) can be achieved'* I really appreciate the clever and cautious way that Bill words things, always leaving a way out for me. He also talks about 'perfectionist dreams,' and boy do we have them, and if we've learnt one painful thing in sobriety it's that we are not perfect. Nor does God want us to be. Our perfectionism, should it ever miraculously occur, would make God redundant, so until then, let's continue to lean on His perfect ideals and when we are able, practice these principles in all our affairs.

So to finally sum up, just for today we're doing ok. We are human. Today love may be hidden by a shadow and hard to see or feel. Or it may well be bright and visible, as strong as steel, fixed and unbending. Some days we may want to let go, another, to keep holding on. If we are ever in doubt, we can always do what we did in the beginning and ask for help. What is important is that with help we strive to move forward in what is a very difficult and demanding world.

The End

This book is published by Futurus Books.
More information about the writings of
Chris Sharpe can be found at:

www.futurusbooks.co.uk

FuturusBooks

Printed in Great Britain
by Amazon

44716238R00067